# SAVING
# GRACE

A ( 4-WEEK ) STUDY

## DAN BOONE

THE FOUNDRY
PUBLISHING®

Copyright © 2023 by The Foundry Publishing®
The Foundry Publishing
PO Box 419527
Kansas City, MO 64141
thefoundrypublishing.com

978-0-8341-4193-3

Printed in the
United States of America

Cover design: Rob Monacelli
Interior design: Sharon Page

Library of Congress Cataloging-in-Publication Data
A complete catalog record for this book is available from the Library of
Congress.

The internet addresses, email addresses, and phone numbers in this book
are accurate at the time of publication. They are provided as a resource. The
Foundry Publishing does not endorse them or vouch for their content or
permanence.

10 9 8 7 6 5 4 3 2 1

# CONTENTS

## WEEK 1

# THE HUMAN CHASE

I like theological movies. A theological movie is not necessarily an overtly Christian or religious movie but simply one that is cut from the cloth of the biblical narrative. My wife says I can't watch a movie without performing a theological autopsy on it. Having spent much of my life studying and preaching the Christ story, I do tend to interpret anything I see through the lens of this grand life narrative. I see the movie characters as humans who are on a quest for something—and that something, even if they don't realize it, is their own humanity. They are trying to figure out how to live in their own skin as fully human creatures—the people they were meant to be.

Deep within us all, there is a sense of destiny, calling, purpose, and meaning. We grouse about trying to find this key to life. I call it "the human chase." One of the best movies about the human chase is *Groundhog Day*. Bill Murray stars as a reporter who is assigned to Punxsutawney, Pennsylvania, to cover the appearance of the nationally famous groundhog, Punxsutawney Phil. While there, Murray's character gets stuck in a loop and is forced to relive the same day over and over and over. Every morning when he wakes up, it is Groundhog Day all over again.

Here he is, this fragile creature stuck in time and feeling the futility of trying every way he knows to get into a meaningful tomorrow, but nothing changes his circumstances. He tries a variety of approaches throughout the movie: using people, avoiding people, manipulating people, hurting people, hurting himself, and more. Even-

5

We could also view *Groundhog Day* as a modern-day parable of Ecclesiastes.

tually he decides to try a new tactic, and he awakes to the joy of serving, the beauty of giving, the love of music and art, and the capacity to love. Only then does he succeed in waking up into tomorrow.

*Groundhog Day* and its concluding moral remind me of the God who stands on the threshold of tomorrow, waiting as we chase our meaning until we run headlong into the grace that was there waiting all the time. We could also view *Groundhog Day* as a modern-day parable of Ecclesiastes. In his translation of the book of Ecclesiastes in The Message, Eugene Peterson has explained his translation choice for the word "Ecclesiastes" itself, which is traditionally translated as something like "preacher" or "teacher": "Because of the experiential stance of the writing in [Ecclesiastes], giving voice to what is so basic among men and women throughout history, I have translated [the word 'Ecclesiastes'] 'the Quester.'"[1] He also writes in the Ecclesiastes introduction about the ultimately futile human impulse to search for and make our own meaning out of life:

> Ecclesiastes is a famous—maybe the world's most famous—witness to this experience of futility. The acerbic wit catches our attention. The stark honesty compels notice. And people do notice—oh, how they notice! Nonreligious and religious alike notice. Unbe-

---

1. Eugene Peterson, "Introduction: Ecclesiastes," *The Message: The Bible in Contemporary Language* (Colorado Springs, CO: Navpress, 2002), 1163.

lievers and believers notice. More than a few of them are surprised to find this kind of thing in the Bible.

But it is most emphatically and necessarily in the Bible in order to call a halt to our various and futile attempts to make something of our lives, so that we can give our full attention to God—who God is and what he does to make something of us. Ecclesiastes actually doesn't say that much about God; the author leaves that to the other sixty-five books of the Bible. His task is to expose our total incapacity to find the meaning and completion of our lives on our own.

It is our propensity to go off on our own, trying to be human by our own devices and desires, that makes Ecclesiastes necessary reading. Ecclesiastes sweeps our souls clean of all "lifestyle" spiritualities so that we can be ready for God's visitation revealed in Jesus Christ. Ecclesiastes is a John-the-Baptist kind of book. It functions not as a meal but as a bath. It is not nourishment; it is cleansing. It is repentance. It is purging. We read Ecclesiastes to get scrubbed clean from illusion and sentiment, from ideas that are idolatrous and feelings that cloy. It is an exposé and rejection of every arrogant and ignorant expectation that we can live our lives by ourselves on our own terms.[2]

---

2. Peterson, "Introduction: Ecclesiastes," *The Message*, 1162–63.

Eugene Peterson's translation of Ecclesiastes begins like this:

> These are the words of the Quester, David's son and king in Jerusalem: Smoke, nothing but smoke. There's nothing to anything—it's all smoke. What's there to show for a lifetime of work, a lifetime of working your fingers to the bone? One generation goes its way, the next one arrives, but nothing changes—it's business as usual for old planet earth.
>
> What was will be again, what happened will happen again. There's nothing new on this earth.
>
> Call me "the Quester." I've been king over Israel in Jerusalem. I looked most carefully into everything, searched out all that is done on this earth. And let me tell you, there's not much to write home about. God hasn't made it easy for us. I've seen it all and it's nothing but smoke—smoke, and spitting into the wind. (1:1–4, 9, 12–14)

How's that for good news? Cynicism and the futility of the human quest for meaning are the largest themes in the book of Ecclesiastes. The writer's favorite word is the Hebrew word *hebel*, which is translated "smoke, fog, vapor," "vanity," or "meaninglessness." *Hebel* is the idea that you reach for something of substance only to find that, when you catch it and close your fingers around it, it has already disappeared into thin air. Chasing the meaning of life on our own is like trying to hold fog in our hands. It is here today and gone tomorrow. Like *Groundhog Day*, the author in Ecclesiastes says we keep repeating the same chase day after day and waking up with nothing of substance.

Part of me wants to argue with the author when he writes about "nothing new under the sun" (v. 9). He just doesn't understand the progress of humanity! We have coffee that is fresh when we wake up; we have self-driving cars; we have lights that go on when we enter a room; we have entire libraries on a flash drive. There's something new every day! There has never been a time on the planet when humans were more surrounded by new things. Yet we still wake up every morning believing there is something more we must chase and catch and consume that will bring fulfillment. Our friend in Ecclesiastes, the Quester, tells us he chased money and power and work and pleasure and knowledge and youth; caught them, owned them, consumed them—and woke up the next morning clutching fog. Is the human meant to be nothing more than a restless chaser?

Genesis 2:7 says, "Then the LORD God formed man from the dust of the ground and breathed [*ruach*] into his nostrils the breath [*ruach*] of life, and the man became a living being [*nephesh*]." We begin as lumps of clay, the dust of the earth. God, in the language of Genesis, leans over our inanimate bodies and blows divine breath into our nose. The Hebrew word for "breath" is the same as the word for "spirit" or "wind." Throughout our story, divine wind, or breath, is the energizing activity of God. It is what comes upon prophets. It is what falls upon the baptized

Throughout our story,
divine wind, or breath,
is the energizing
activity of God.

Jesus. It is what fills the upper room in Acts. It is divine wind and breath—or Holy Spirit. Human life exists as the gift of God's breath.

I have been in birthing rooms and dying rooms. When a child emerges from a mother's womb, the first instinct is to gasp for air. The instant the baby breathes for the first time, skin color changes, lungs expand, a body cries out. The first gulp of air is always *in*—as if waiting for God to blow life into the nostrils. In the dying rooms, as saints take their last breath, the final breath is always out. No one inhales and then dies. We exhale when we expire. The breath returns to the God who gave it. We are sustained not by something we chase and catch but by the gift of God.

The Genesis text says that humanity became "living beings" (*nephesh* in the Hebrew) when God breathed life into us. *Nephesh* is an interesting word that basically means "throat." The throat is a passageway from inside to outside. And it is located in the most vulnerable part of the body—the neck. Through this portal passes all that is needed to keep us alive: water, air, food. In a sense, the human is a walking hunger, a talking thirst, an aching need. We are not self-sustained but needy creatures. To be human is to be vulnerable, needy, dependent, desiring, hungry, fragile. And, like our friend in *Groundhog Day*, we chase anything that fills the gnawing in our gut—money, position, fame, power, sex, acclaim, body image, attention, anything. We are desiring beings.

Christians have at times forgotten the essence of our human neediness and have preached a gospel that says our desires are wrong and should be suppressed or denied. But we can't do that because desiring is the very *essence* of our humanity. Our problem is not *that* we desire but *what* we desire. Our desires, when we live apart from God, are twisted, bent inward, and focused on self-saving quests.

Let's talk about another old Bill Murray movie, *What about Bob?* This time Murray plays Bob, a fragile human who has every phobia, mental illness, and problem he can think of. He is a walking mess. He has driven one counselor from the profession entirely and is referred to Dr. Leo Marvin, a self-assured therapist who has written a book, *Baby Steps*, that is supposed to solve all human problems. His clients simply need to take baby steps out of their problems and into wholeness. Bob latches onto Dr. Marvin as his new hope. When he learns that Dr. Marvin has gone on a family vacation, he conspires to find out where he is. Bob's arrival at the vacation site coincides with Dr. Marvin's exit from a store on Main Street. Bob is scolded for inappropriately interrupting the family and is told to go home. He drops to his knees and becomes the best demonstration of a human that I have ever seen. He simply says, "I need. I need. I need." This is what it means to be human.

When John Wesley was asked what is the most perfect creature of all, he supposedly responded, "A void, capable of being filled with God, by God." We are made

13

with the capacity to receive life as a gift from God, not only in the form of physical breath but also in the form of saving grace. "As a deer longs for flowing streams, so my soul longs for you, O God. My soul thirsts for God, for the living God" (Psalm 42:1–2a). Thus we sing in the hymn "O Worship the King": "Frail children of dust and feeble as frail, in thee do we trust nor find thee to fail. Thy mercies how tender, how firm to the end! Our Maker, Defender, Redeemer, and Friend."[3]

---

3. Johann Michael Haydn (music, 18th c.), William Gardiner (music arr., 1815), and Robert Grant (words, 1833), "O Worship the King," *Sing to the Lord: Hymnal* (Kansas City, MO: Lillenas Publishing Co., 1993), #64.

# JOURNALING AND REFLECTION

Pause to reflect on what you have read. What did you hear? Restate it in your own words. Make it your own. What is God pointing out in this chapter for you to think more about? What is God saying to you?

_____

_____

_____

_____

_____

_____

_____

_____

_____

_____

_____

_____

_____

_____

# PRAYER

Thank God in your own words for creating you with the capacity to receive divine breath and life. Express your utter dependence on God. Embrace your fragile, needy humanity.

# DISCUSSION

1. At the end of *What About Bob?*, the therapist who did so much to help Bob, Dr. Marvin, ends up constrained in a straitjacket in a psych ward while Bob ends up full of life. What do you think this ending is trying to say?

2. How is our world perfectly wired to enable a lifetime of chasing?

3. How would you explain saving grace to someone who struggles with the human chase?

4. Why are money, sex, power, attention, success—and whatever else we chase—never enough?

5. What does it mean to "be at home in our own skin" and what does that have to do with saving grace?

NOTES

# THE "S" WORD

In the past, the word "sex" was a whispered word. It was rarely spoken out loud in public. It was often called the "S" word. But times have changed, and now that word is everywhere in every form. Sex is no longer the "S" word. It has been replaced by another word that, if mentioned at all, is whispered or spoken in muted tones. That word is *sin*. Saying "sin" out loud in public is like saying "bomb" in an airport. People get very uncomfortable, and you may be in for some intense scrutiny. So we don't say it! We say other words instead, like *blunder, mistake, wrong, foible, infraction, error in judgment, flaw, weakness,* or *shortcoming.* If sin, like some ancient diseases, had disappeared from the face of the earth, maybe our choice not to say it would be fine. But the last time I checked, we aren't living in Eden, and sin is still among us.

Somewhere, within an hour of where you are, a spouse is cheating, a suspect is evading capture, a thief is stealing, a politician is lying, an athlete is using PEDs, a student is plagiarizing, an insurance company is denying a fair claim, a manufacturer is polluting, an addict is gambling, a preacher is abusing trust, a churchgoer is withholding God's tithe, or a builder is cutting a corner. Sometimes these things are reported, and sometimes they are swept under the rug. But rarely does anyone use the term "sin" to speak about them. Sin is the new "S" word.

To be honest, sin is a slippery word. It is hard to nail down with an exact definition. There are about twenty different words in both Hebrew and Greek. The range of

Theologians have more kinds of sin than Bubba Gump has shrimp.

meanings include iniquity, guilt, transgression, intentional wrong, willful rebellion, missing the mark, inequity, and lots of other biblical concepts. Theologians have more kinds of sin than Bubba Gump has shrimp: original sin, individual sin, corporate sin, willful sin, high-handed sin, unpardonable sin, sins of omission, sins of commission, social sin, domestic sin, mortal sin, venial sin, sins of ignorance, seven deadly sins. There doesn't seem to be a shortage of sin for the foreseeable future. But another problem is that different religious groups call different things sin. We have a hard time agreeing about what goes on the list and what doesn't. What may be sin to one isn't to another.

Our world has even organized its occupations to counter sin. To educators, sin is an issue of values clarification, cultural enlightenment, and diversity training. To biologists, sin is hard-wired in the genes we are born with. To politicians, sin is in the social systems, and we solve it by electing the right people and passing the right laws. To police, sin is the darkness that must be confronted with law and order. To psychologists, sin is understandable and predictable given what has been done to us, and we need therapy, self-awareness, and maybe medication. To social justice leaders, sin is combated with protest, compassion, and reform. To moralists, sin is solved if we all play nice, share, practice positivity, and do what Oprah says. To TV preachers, sin is solved by laying our hands on the TV, sending money, and claiming our miracle. To advertisers, sin dissolves with the purchase of a new product. Some of these approaches are helpful, and some are not.

So what do we do? We find a friend in Psalm 32 who is wrestling with this same question:

> Happy are those whose transgression is forgiven, whose sin is covered. Happy are those to whom the LORD imputes no iniquity and in whose spirit there is no deceit. While I kept silent, my body wasted away through my groaning all day long. For day and night your hand was heavy upon me; my strength was dried up as by the heat of summer. Then I acknowledged my sin to you, and I did not hide my iniquity. I said, "I will confess my transgressions to the LORD," and you forgave the guilt of my sin. Therefore let all who are faithful offer prayer to you; at a time of distress, the rush of mighty waters shall not reach them. You are a hiding place for me; you preserve me from trouble; you surround me with glad cries of deliverance.
> (Psalm 32:1–7)

The psalmist suggests that keeping our sin pent up inside causes our body to waste away. Sin eats at our bones, causes us to groan our way through each day, is a heavy weight, and feels like being swept away in a flood to certain destruction. So the psalmist acknowledges his sin rather than hiding it, confessing transgression to the Lord. The result is happiness, forgiveness, and deliverance. The "S" word becomes an honest confession in the presence of the God of saving grace. If we never confront the reality

If we never confront the reality of our sin, there is no solution for it.

of our sin, there is no solution for it. God is the only place where our sin can be taken and confessed with the hope of being restored. We need to recover the language of sin if we hope to be saved.

I suggest a robust theology of sin—but humbly spoken. Some denounce sin with self-righteous condemnation, sounding like Oscar the Sanctified Grouch. On the other hand, others have stopped saying the word altogether because it makes people uncomfortable. David Brooks, an op-ed columnist for the *New York Times*, writes in *Road to Character,*

> In many times and many places, the word sin was used to declare war on pleasure, even on the healthy pleasures of sex and entertainment. Sin was used as a pretext to live joylessly and censoriously. . . . The word sin was abused by the self-righteous, by dry-hearted souls who seemed alarmed by the possibility that someone somewhere might be enjoying himself. . . . But in truth, sin is one of those words that is impossible to do without. Sin is a necessary piece of our mental furniture because it reminds us that life is a moral affair. Sin is baked into our nature and is handed down through the generations. We are all sinners together.[1]

---

1. David Brooks, *The Road to Character* (New York: Random House, 2015), 53–54.

Brooks is right. The word "sin" is necessary when we talk about the human condition, but we need to speak of sin with the humble recognition that it has lived in our own houses. Later in the book, Brooks comes very near the Wesleyan understanding of sin when he suggests that it is a loyalty to a lower love. Sin represents our capacity to love bent inward on the self. It is self-sovereignty, self-deception, and self-rule all rolled up into one, and it devastates us and those we love.

Barbara Brown Taylor writes,

The days are long gone when most preachers can stand up in pulpits and name people's sins for them. They do not have that authority anymore. What they *can* do, I believe, is to describe the experience of sin and its aftermath so vividly that people can identify its presence in their own lives, not as a chronic source of guilt, nor as sure proof that they are inherently bad, but as the part of their individual and corporate lives that is crying out for change. . . . Sin is our only hope, because the recognition that something is wrong is the first step toward setting it right again. There is no help for those who admit no need of help. There is no repair for those who insist that nothing is broken, and there is no hope of transformation for a world whose inhabitants accept that it is sadly but irreversibly wrecked.[2]

Maybe it is time to revive the "S" word, in humble tones, for the sake of our salvation. The grand news of the gospel is that saving grace is present at the very point of human confession—and our God saves!

2. Barbara Brown Taylor, *Speaking of Sin: The Lost Language of Salvation* (Cambridge, MA: Cowley Publications, 2000), 57–59.

# JOURNALING AND REFLECTION

Pause to reflect on what you have read. What did you hear? Restate it in your own words. Make it your own. What is God pointing out in this chapter for you to think more about? What is God saying to you?

_____

_____

_____

_____

_____

_____

_____

_____

_____

_____

_____

_____

_____

_____

# PRAYER

Rather than writing your own prayer today, spend time in the following confession from the *Book of Common Prayer.*

*Almighty God, to whom all hearts are open, all desires known, and from whom no secrets are hidden: cleanse the thoughts of our hearts by the inspiration of your Holy Spirit, that we may perfectly love you, and worthily magnify your holy name; through Christ our Lord. Amen.*

# DISCUSSION

1. How do you define sin?

2. In your circle of friends, what would happen if you asked during a casual meal, "What do you think about sin?"

3. Why have we started to avoid the word "sin" in our larger culture?

4. We believe that sin is both personal and corporate—
present in the human heart *and* in institutional systems.
Which is easiest to identify in our current culture?

5. How familiar are you with the practice of confession,
and how often do you do it?

# NOTES

## WEEK 3

# THE POWER OF FORGIVENESS

We become profoundly human when we realize that we are needy and pray, "Give us this day our daily bread." We become even more human when we are willing to confess that we were wrong, that we have sinned, and that we need forgiveness. Asking for forgiveness humbles us. It places us at the mercy of another who is empowered either to forgive or to hold back forgiveness. God has given us the assurance that if we confess our sins, he will be faithful and just to forgive us. Saving grace is *forgiving* grace.

I suppose the Lord's Prayer would be easier to pray if it stopped with, "Forgive us our trespasses," but it goes on to say, "as we forgive those who trespass against us." Does that mean God won't forgive us until we forgive? Does it mean we *earn* our forgiveness from God by forgiving? Does it mean we have to sweep horrible wrongs under the rug and look the other way as if they never happened, or God won't forgive us? These misinterpretations of forgiveness do great damage to the justice of God. Forgiveness is not meant to dull our capacity to be angry at sinful behavior. Biblical justice matters, especially if the kingdom of God is to come among us.

So let's look at being forgi*ven* in connection with being forgi*ving*. Let's say someone has really sinned against you—lied about you, stolen from you, taken advantage of you, raped you, cheated on you, intentionally hurt you—and any other sins you want to throw on this pile. Is the

35

Anger liberates us from denial, and forgiveness moves the relationship toward restoration rather than destruction.

Lord's Prayer saying we just forgive and forget and go on as if nothing happened? No.

Before we can think of forgiving a bully, a brute, or a beast, we need to thank God for the grace to be angry. We need to get our arms around the reality that this is not how God intended it to be. Making nice and acting like it didn't cause harm does not benefit the harmer or the harmed. And it hinders the kind of peacemaking that God is after. *The first step in forgiveness is to acknowledge that wrong has been done to you and that you are angry about it.*

I find great comfort in Paul's instruction to the Ephesians when he says, "Be angry but do not sin" (4:26). That's all the permission I need to be genuinely bothered about what was done to me. This is good anger, the anger that calls sin what it is, the kind of anger that stands for biblical justice and is willing to confront rather than ignore. Once we get this right, we can move toward forgiveness—not as the *end* of anger but as the *transformation* of our anger for the good of the person who wronged us. Anger liberates us from denial, and forgiveness moves the relationship toward restoration rather than destruction.

Now let me go a step further. In forgiving this person, I don't think we excuse the person for what was done. We do not experience God's forgiveness unless we repent. God's posture is forgiveness. This is a finished act that flows from saving grace and is completed in the cross and resurrection of Jesus. If we confess our sins, he is faithful and just to forgive us. God has already made the decision

37

to forgive, has already provided the forgiveness, has already taken the posture of forgiveness, has already promised us the forgiveness, but *until we confess the sin and commit to changing* (because "repent" literally means to turn around and go the other direction), we cannot experience the forgiveness of God. Neither can the person who has wronged us be truly forgiven until they acknowledge the wrong and repent.

I remember the first time I kissed my wife, Denise. It was several dates into our budding relationship. I had dreamed about it, hoped for it. I even caught myself practicing in front of the bathroom mirror. Lame, I know. It takes two to experience a kiss. For one to say, "I stand ready to kiss you" is movement in the right direction. But if the other does not also lean in or agree to the kiss, there is no kiss. It takes two for the experience to be fulfilled and enjoyed.

Even if we stand ready to forgive, forgiveness cannot be fully realized until the one who did us wrong leans into the kiss of forgiveness, enabling a restored relationship. Does this mean we are to carry a grudge and withhold forgiveness from the jerk until they 'fess up? No. We are to forgive *as God forgives*, which means we take in our hearts a posture of willingness to forgive. We no longer hold an offender in our mental jail, waiting for them to appear in our court of judgment. We no longer grill them over the fire of our anger. We no longer carry them around, trying to get them to admit wrong, or hating them for not doing so. Instead, we turn them over to God for justice to be done. We, like God, stand ready to forgive. Revenge and justice belong to God. When we forgive, even if it's before the other person has sincerely repented, we release them to God for God to do with them as God sees fit, believing that God is both just and merciful.

Christians are called to live into forgiveness willingly, in the same way that God is graciously forgiving. Then we can go on. We release the issue and the person to God, realizing that if we do not, we will become imprisoned by bitterness, resentment, and hatred. It's a horrible thing to experience wrong at the hands of others, but it's far worse to imprison ourselves over it our inability to forgive. In Christ, we lay the burden down. When we learn to forgive, it feels like unloading a fifty-pound backpack after a fifteen-mile hike.

But there is still another connection between being forgiven by God and being forgiving toward others. Following the Matthew version of the Lord's Prayer, there is even a postscript about forgiveness: "For if you forgive others their trespasses, your heavenly Father will also forgive you, but if you do not forgive others, neither will your Father forgive your trespasses" (Matthew 6:14-15). What is being said here? Sometimes the best way to understand one scripture is with another scripture.

In Matthew 18, Peter is asking Jesus how many times he must forgive someone. He even suggests an answer to Jesus he feels is generous: seven times. Since seven in the Bible is the perfect, whole, complete number, this

Sometimes the best way to understand one scripture is with another scripture.

ought to be enough! He may think Jesus will congratulate him on being so magnanimous. Then kapow! Jesus raises the ante. Not seven times, but seventy *times* seven—or seventy-seven times, depending on the translation. Either way, both numbers are a lot higher than seven. But the real answer to Peter's question is not in the number but in the parable that follows (vv. 23–35).

It goes like this. A king decides to collect on his debts and calls in all those who owe him money. A man comes in who owes the king ten thousand talents. Let's pause to do a little math. One talent back then was equivalent to about fifteen *years* of full-time salary. So this guy would need to work 150,000 years *and* turn over every cent he earned in order to pay off the debt—and that's assuming there's no interest accumulation. The people hearing this parable would've known right away that it would be mathematically impossible for this man to pay his debt. He owed more than the entire wealth of some nations! It would be like if someone today owed the amount of the U.S. national debt (which is up in the trillions).

The king announces his debt, and the servant says he doesn't have it and cannot pay it. The king responds very coldly, without even seeming to look up. The king essentially says to the guards, "Liquidate him. Sell his wife, his kids, his house, have a big garage sale, everything goes! Then throw him in prison until he can pay off the remaining balance. Next!" This action is both swift and fair. He owes, and he can't pay. The king's decision is just.

But the guy falls to his knees and says to the king, "Have patience with me, and I will pay you everything" (v. 26). The Greek word for what he is asking is *makrothuméson*. It is translated "patience." It's what an old but good song from my youth was talking about: "Give me just a little more time." The king then does three unbelievable things: he has compassion on the servant, he cancels the entire debt, and he lets the servant go free.

Remember, this is a parable that Jesus started telling in order to illustrate an answer to Peter's question about how many times God expects us to forgive. Jesus says the kingdom of heaven is like the merciful king in the parable who cancels a debt that cannot be paid. We know about this forgiving God whose saving grace is beyond our calculation. We've read about him in Scripture: "The LORD is merciful and gracious, slow to anger and abounding in steadfast love. He will not always accuse, nor will he keep his anger forever. He does not deal with us according to our sins nor repay us according to our iniquities" (Psalm 103:8–10).

Jesus is painting a portrait of the forgiving Father for his disciples—but pictures don't always reveal everything. Over our fireplace we have a family portrait. All seventeen of us are in it: four married couples and eight grandchildren. It was taken in the fall out in our backyard. We are all dressed casually. I had just come from a Tennessee Titans football game. I had on jeans, a sweatshirt, white socks, and tennis shoes. I was sitting cross-legged on the ground for the photo. Denise, my wife, did not like the idea of my white socks shining brilliantly in the middle of the picture. So I gathered fall leaves and piled them around my feet, hiding the white socks. But my white socks are not the only things hidden. There are baby bottles, pacifiers, ball caps, and diaper bags strategically hidden behind the backs of parents and spouses. The messy stuff is hidden.

It's easy for us to look at this parable and see a king loaded with the wealth of the world. He won't miss it if this guy can't pay. He's like the Texas oil tycoon who gets in his long Cadillac with steer horns on the hood and drives out to the far edge of his thousand-acre spread, struts over to a struggling tenant farmer, and announces in his thick Texas drawl, "I'm gonna give you this little plot of land you've been farming," and then gets back in his Cadillac and drives off into the sunset. This sort of generosity would cost the Texas oil tycoon nothing—or at least nothing he'll notice.

Don't take that picture of God. Beneath the regal robe of this saving grace King is a cross-shaped scar, a hidden reminder of the cost of forgiveness. It is not obvious in the parable, but it is an essential part of the portrait of who God is. Yes, God is generous because God has much to be generous with—but do not for a moment think that God's generous mercy did not cost him something.

The king cancels the debt. He sets the servant free. Let's follow the forgiven servant and see what he does: "But when that servant went out, he found one of his

fellow servants who owed him a hundred silver coins"
(Matthew 18:28a, NIV). Helpful note: the amount owed in
this scripture (a hundred silver coins, or a hundred denarii,
depending on translation) is equal to roughly ten bucks.
"He grabbed him and began to choke him. 'Pay back what
you owe me!' he demanded. His fellow servant fell to his
knees and begged him, 'Be patient with me, and I will pay
it back.' But he refused. Instead, he went off and had the
man thrown into prison until he could pay the debt" (vv.
28b–30, NIV).

Wouldn't you love to be this guy's friend? He's living
like he still owes the debt, and if he has to pay, *so does
everyone else*. The saddest thing about the story is that he
doesn't behave as if he's been forgiven. Maybe he didn't
hear the king correctly. Maybe he is under the impression
that he got what he asked for—*makrothuméson*—more time
to pay the debt. He has his brother by the throat demanding
that ten bucks or else, an amount that is certainly repay-
able, given a little more time. This wrong can be righted. But
instead of compassion that mirrors the compassion the king
has just shown him, he delivers swift, immediate justice. Off
to jail you go, brother!

Look what happens next: "When the other servants saw
what had happened, they were outraged and went and told
their master everything that had happened. Then the master
called the servant in. 'You wicked servant,' he said, 'I canceled
all that debt of yours because you begged me to. Shouldn't
you have had mercy on your fellow servant just as I had on

you?' In anger his master handed him over to the jailers to be tortured, until he should pay back all he owed" (vv. 31–34, NIV).

The refusal to forgive is too great a torture for humans to bear. It is a self-imposed prison. When the king forgave the debt, the servant walked away owing *almost* nothing. He did still owe something that only the forgiven can pay, something the Lord's Prayer calls us to do. What we owe God for our forgiveness is *resemblance*, or *mirroring*—to forgive in the same way that we have been forgiven. We are empowered by the Spirit of God to resemble and mirror God by taking the posture of forgiveness in the same way it has been modeled for and extended to us.

# JOURNALING AND REFLECTION

Pause to reflect on what you have read. What did you hear? Restate it in your own words. Make it your own. What is God pointing out in this chapter for you to think more about? What is God saying to you?

_____

_____

_____

_____

_____

_____

_____

_____

_____

_____

_____

_____

_____

_____

# PRAYER

Write your prayer to God comparing the wrong that has been done to you to the wrong that you have done to God and others. Imagine the debt that you owe God. How does your forgiveness of others resemble God's forgiveness of you?

# DISCUSSION

1. How is it possible to be angry yet not sin against those who have harmed us?

2. How does your forgiveness resemble God's forgiveness?

3. What is the relationship between forgiveness and saving grace?

4. How does your awareness of sins committed against you by others help you understand the way God deals with your sins?

5. Why is the forgiveness of saving grace a liberating experience? What happens inside a forgiven person?

## WEEK 4

# ATONEMENT

When we think about grace as the gift of God, we recognize that it comes in many forms. Prevenient grace is the searching grace of God that has always been present, even before we knew we needed it. It waits for us in the next moment as a gift that opens us to saving grace. As we yield to prevenient grace, a relationship with God through saving grace becomes possible. The Bible uses many metaphors to describe the gift of saving grace.

Saving grace is like being born again, brought from no life, to life in Christ.

Saving grace is like being set free from bondage to sin.

Saving grace is like being adopted into a family.

Saving grace is like becoming a citizen of a new regime—the kingdom of God.

Saving grace is like being made right by the gracious act of another.

Saving grace is like being bought out of a debt that we could not repay.

Saving grace is like being reconciled to someone from whom we were estranged.

Saving grace is like turning around in the middle of the road and heading the opposite direction.

Saving grace is like being found when we were helplessly lost.

Saving grace is like coming home.

Saving grace is like a cleansing bath.

Saving grace is like a fresh start.

━━━━━━

Atonement is sometimes rightly defined as *at-one-ment*—the act of God that reconciles us to God, or makes us one with God.

━━━━━━

Saving grace is like a new covenant agreement that establishes a new relationship with new terms for living.

The metaphors could go on because the experience of new life in Christ begs for descriptions that can capture the wonder and beauty of a gift that transforms and reorders our lives. One of the prominent biblical themes that underlies saving grace is *atonement*. This act of a sacrifice on our behalf that brings forgiveness of sin and reconciliation of relationship is a primary story in Scripture. It is an act of God by which we are brought near to God, our sins forgiven and our defilements cleansed. Atonement restores our relationship with God. Atonement is sometimes rightly defined as *at-one-ment*—the act of God that reconciles us to God, or makes us one with God.

Paul writes these things in his second letter to the Corinthian church:

- "For the love of Christ urges us on, because we are convinced that one has died for all; therefore all have died. And he died for all, so that those who live might live no longer for themselves but for the one who for their sake died and was raised" (5:14–15).
- "So if anyone is in Christ, there is a new creation: everything old has passed away; look, new things have come into being!" (v. 17).
- "In Christ God was reconciling the world to himself, not counting their trespasses against them" (v. 19a).

53

- "For our sake God made the one who knew no sin to be sin, so that in him we might become the righteousness of God" (v. 21).

This language is rooted in the Old Testament understanding of sacrifice. The phrases in this New Testament text are expressions of what was once done to an animal but now has been accomplished for the final time in Jesus's death:

- "One has died" is what happened at the temple altar with animals—one animal sacrificed for many sins.
- "Not counting their trespasses against them" is what occurred in the process of sacrifices offered for sin.
- "God made the one who knew no sin to be sin" is the reality of a blameless animal being sacrificed on behalf of guilty humans.
- Becoming righteous is the gift of God to restore us to right relationship by way of the faithful offering of another.
- "Everything old has passed away" signaled the new relationship between God and those offering sacrifice for their sins.

The Old Testament sacrifices were the means set forth by God to establish and preserve a covenant relationship that accounted for the sins of the people. Sacrifice was how they repented and turned from their sins toward God. It was how they recognized that they were responsi-

ble for their sins and that they bore a cost, a debt, a yield-
ing up of something blameless that would be acceptable
to God. It was how their contamination of the relationship
was made right and the community made clean again. It
was how relationship was restored between themselves
and others and also between themselves and God. It was
the covenant practice that enabled a holy God to be present among a sinful people. While this was the act of the
people through a priest, it was not human action in making the sacrifice that mattered but God's action in receiv-
ing the sacrifice that effected the change. Sacrifice was the
merciful pathway of God's saving grace.

The high point of the sacrificial system was the Day
of Atonement. On this day, the whole of Israel's sin was
atoned for—willful or accidental, known or unknown. In
one offering, all the sin of all the people was brought before God and atoned for. Every year, the entire community
gathered as the high priest made atoning sacrifices for the
whole community. As the post-resurrection followers of
Jesus (some of whom were Jewish followers of God before Jesus arrived, remember) read the book of Leviticus,
they started to see the crucifixion of Jesus in light of the
Day of Atonement. We find four strands of thought emerg-
ing in the New Testament that are directly connected to
the ancient practice of atonement.

## Strand 1: A Debt Owed

Many of our traditional hymns and songs reflect the thought that Jesus paid our debt, covered our sin, offered up what we could not in exchange for our forgiveness. It is important to note what this means and what it doesn't mean. There are multiple theories of atonement out there. One is called "penal satisfaction" and portrays God as an angry party demanding payment in exchange for forgiveness. Imagine an angry parent saying someone will be spanked for the broken lamp and waiting for someone to step forward and take the beating. To picture the Father in this way is to forget that a loving God is one who *offers* the sacrifice. God was *in Christ* reconciling us to himself. This is not a picture of a God who waits for us to produce repayment but a God who moves to provide repayment.

Another important distinction in the language of debt owed is that atonement "covers our sin." This language has often been misunderstood as masking or veiling our sin from God. This line of thought suggests that a holy God cannot look upon sin without destroying its carriers. Some have interpreted the Father's abandonment of his Son on the cross as God turning his back because Jesus bears the sin of the world and the holy God cannot bear to look upon sin. The proof text used for this interpretation is the Psalm 22 prayer that Jesus utters from the cross: *My God, my God, why have you forsaken me?* There are other, more helpful ways of interpreting this utterance from Jesus, however. Does the Father turn away from the

═══════════

# Love doesn't always look away from things that are hard to see.

═══════════

Son because he bears our sin? I've been with parents in birthing rooms when their babies have come out with disfigurements or other health-related issues, and I've never seen a single parent look away from the child they love. Love doesn't look away from things that are hard to see. And if God is love, then God doesn't look away either.

I've also heard people say that God does not see our sin when he looks at us because the blood of Jesus is like a blanket that hides our sin from the eyes of a holy God. We have songs about sin that talk about being "covered by the blood." While "to hide from plain sight" is one meaning of the word "cover," it is not a biblical meaning in relation to sin. God sees our sin. God is not trying to hide our sin from God's sight but to cleanse us from our sin. The idea of the blood covering our sin is like someone going to the bank on our behalf and covering our house payment. It is not a covering *up* but a covering *on behalf of.* This distinction is important because we must understand what happens after we are saved. We are not saved to keep on being sinners whose sins are concealed from God. We are saved to be set free from the burden and power of sin. It is not an imagined restoration but a real one.

## Strand 2: Cleansing

We are washed in the blood, cleansed of defilement, made pure. In the Old Testament atonement rituals, the sprinkling of blood in certain places in the temple was considered an act of purification. When we read the letter to the Hebrews in the New Testament, it becomes clear that blood as purification and cleansing is the dominant way that the writer understands atonement. Jesus is the better sacrifice, the once-and-forever sacrifice, whose blood accomplishes what the repeated animal sacrifices of the Old Testament system could never fully and finally accomplish—the definitive cleansing of sin forever. As the old hymn says, "What can wash away my sin? Nothing but the blood of Jesus!"

Saving grace is the loving act of God by which our sinful filth and contamination are washed away, leaving us pure and clean in the presence of God. That is why baptism is viewed as a washing that ushers us into new life.

## Strand 3: Repentance

The word "repentance" means to stop moving in the direction you are going, intentionally turn around, and go in the opposite direction. As self-sovereign sinners, we have charted our own path walking rebelliously before God. In the act of sacrifice, it becomes clear that our way is the way of death. We accept responsibility for this and turn toward God. Prevenient grace enables us to do this.

## Strand 4: Covenant

Covenant is about the relationship that God desires to have with us. Atonement (at-one-ment) is relational language. The sacrifices are not about business agreements or legal transactions. They are about the restoration of broken relationship. Saving grace is not a thing we get. It is the activity of a God who loves us. God makes a way for us to live in relationship with our Creator, with one another, with ourselves, and within the created world. Atonement makes right relationship possible, and when we experience atonement, we live in peace as faithful and obedient covenant partners.

# JOURNALING AND REFLECTION

Pause to reflect on what you have read. What did you hear? Restate it in your own words. Make it your own. What is God pointing out in this chapter for you to think more about? What is God saying to you?

_____

_____

_____

_____

_____

_____

_____

_____

_____

_____

_____

_____

_____

_____

# PRAYER

Thank God for saving grace in the language of sacrifice. What debt has God covered for you? What contamination has God cleansed from your life? How has your life changed direction in an act of repentance? What does your relationship (or covenant) with God mean to you?

# DISCUSSION

1. Read Hebrews 9:13–14. How is sacrificial language used here?

2. If you were asked, "Why was it necessary for Jesus to die?" how would you answer?

3. Does this chapter's explanation of the blood covering our sin change the way you think about atonement?

4. How would you summarize what you believe about saving grace? What have you learned? What do you celebrate?

# NOTES